Match The Flags

Read and learn about the flags of the United States and the dependencies. Try to remember the colors and design, and their meanings in each flag. Then, find the stamp that matches each flag illustration. Stick the gummed stamp over the illustration.

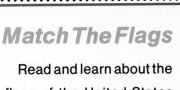

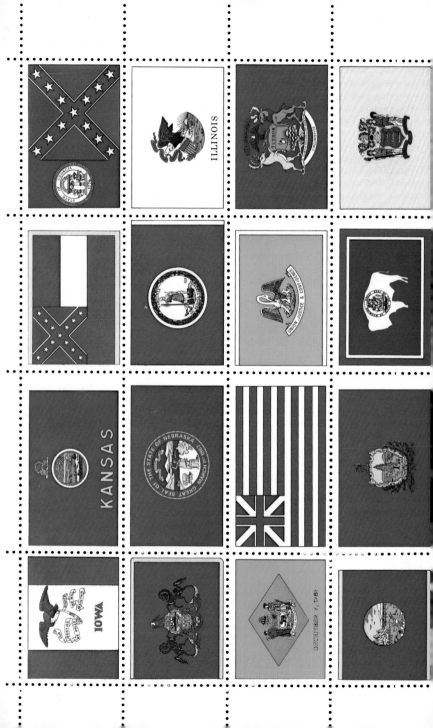

INDIANA
IN GOD WE TRUST
MAY 20th 1775
N C
APRIL 12th 1776
STATE OF OREGON
1859
V I
THE SEAL OF THE STATE OF WASHINGTON 1889

QUI TRANSTULIT SUSTINET
INDUSTRY
UTAH
1847
1896
ARKANSAS
SOUTH DAKOTA
THE SUNSHINE STATE
STATE OF IDAHO
COMMONWEALTH OF KENTUCKY
UNITED WE STAND
DIVIDED WE FALL
OKLAHOMA
BATTLE BORN
CALIFORNIA REPUBLIC

STATE FLAGS

by Janet Adele Bloss

To my camper buddies—Jill, Bruce, Mary, Bob J., Della, Captain Hocking, and Ron

Seventh printing by Willowisp Press 1996.

Published by Willowisp Press
801 94th Avenue North, St. Petersburg, Florida 33702

Printed in the United States of America

8 10 9 7

ISBN 0-87406-183-0

CONTENTS

THE NATIONAL FLAG

The red, white, and blue colors of our national flag were inherited from Great Britain's flag, the *Union Jack*. The Union Jack flew over the colonies, proclaiming Britain's rule until the Revolutionary War.

After the thirteen colonies had claimed their boundaries (but before they rebelled against Great Britain), it was only natural that they would want a flag to represent them as one unit in this new land. Several flags were designed at this time. One of the earliest colonial flags showed thirteen hands pulling an endless chain. Another depicted a fist holding thirteen arrows. There was also a flag portraying a rattlesnake with thirteen rattles on its tail. Thus, the importance of the number thirteen is evident from the very beginning of Colonial times.

But as their relationship with Great Britain grew strained, the colonies hoisted another flag. This flag was called the *Grand Union,* and it was first raised on January 1, 1776. On this same day the formation of the Continental Army was proclaimed. The commander in chief was George Washington, who ultimately led the army to victory over British forces.

The Grand Union flag, which these early patriots

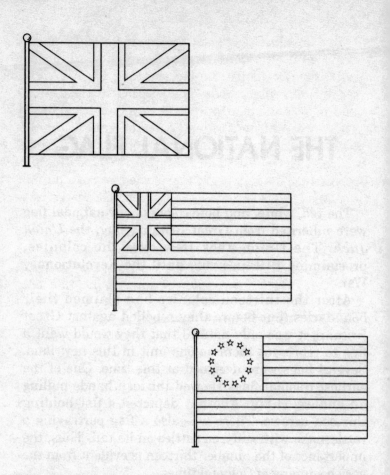

raised, showed six white stripes and seven red stripes representing the thirteen colonies. This same pattern of thirteen stripes is used on the national flag of today. In the Grand Union's upper left corner (the *canton*) was a small flag of England, the Union Jack. Ties, though strained, had not been completely broken with England at this time. The colonists still wanted to recognize their mother country.

But hostilities between the colonists and England grew, and the Continental Congress adopted a resolution to change the flag on June 14, 1777. This resolution replaced the English flag in the Union's canton with thirteen stars against a blue background. There was still no United States of America at this time, and there wouldn't be for another twelve battle-scarred years. But the *Stars and Stripes* of 1777 represented the very beginning of the birth of a nation.

Although the six white and seven red stripes have become standard in today's national flag, the original flag, adopted by the Continental Army, was followed by other flags of varying designs. Some flags used red, white, and blue stripes. Some had a white stripe at the top instead of today's red stripe. Most flag makers, unless instructed *not* to, felt free to add their own ideas to the flag and "improve" it.

Early colonists knew it was important to have a flag because, under international law, a ship at sea without a flag was considered to be a pirate ship. Under this law, anyone with enough power could seize and claim the ship. Thus, from earliest times, flags have served the important function of identification.

When Vermont and Kentucky became the fourteenth and fifteenth states to join the Union, they wanted to be represented by stars on the flag. But some members of Congress didn't want to change the flag. They argued that the idea wasn't even important enough to be discussed. Other people insisted that it *was* important. They wanted each state to have a star. Some argued that it was important for the rest of the world to know that we had two more states plus the original thirteen, and that we were proud of them. And they thought that the new states might be offended by not having their own stars. But others said that there were more important issues at hand than how many stars to put on a flag. The debate raged on.

On January 13, 1794, two stars were added for Vermont and Kentucky and the thirteen stripes were changed to fifteen. But there was still no provision made for how the stars should be arranged. A fifteen-starred flag was flown during the battle over Fort McHenry in the War of 1812, inspiring Francis Scott Key to write "The Star-Spangled Banner." This particular flag was more than forty feet long and had been carefully stitched together by Mary Young Pickersgill and her teenage daughter, Caroline. The flag was too large to fit in the Pickersgills' house, so it was put together at a nearby brewery. This historically rich flag is now on permanent display in the Smithsonian Institution in Washington, D.C.

But a permanent design for the flag was still not official. Flag makers continued to arrange the stars in different patterns in the canton. Some stars were arranged in circles or large star shapes. Other stars were patterned into diamond shapes or ovals. Some were even arranged to form the initials *U.S.* Many divisions in the army didn't use the stars and stripes at all, but designed their own flags instead.

Although the placement of stars on most flags varied throughout the country, the U.S. Navy had already begun to arrange their stars in rows as early as 1777. And for the most part, they stayed with this arrangement. One of the navy's first flags represented the original thirteen states in rows of stars, 3-2-3-2-3.

In 1816, a committee was appointed to decide on a final design for the flag to be used by the entire country. Captain S. C. Reid, a naval officer, suggested to the committee that the stripes be reduced from fifteen to thirteen. He asked that the stars be arranged into one large star on merchant ships carrying goods to other countries. But he wanted the stars to be arranged in parallel lines on warships. Captain Reid also suggested that a star should be added for each new state. But this idea was opposed by other people who thought that even fifteen stars on the flag was too many and that the number of stars should be reduced to the original thirteen.

When Captain Reid made these proposals concerning the flag to Congress, there were twenty states in the Union. But members of Congress still could not agree on the exact specifications for the U.S. flag. And it was not until April 4, 1818, that a bill was passed which stated that the U.S. flag would have thirteen stripes and that each state would be represented by a star. However, the bill again neglected to say *how* the stars should be placed.

By 1857, most ships, but not all, had the stars on their flags arranged into rows. By this time there were thirty states represented by five rows of six stars each. But this arrangement was by no means standard across the nation. Many flags could still be found with the stars arranged in different patterns. The U.S. Navy alone was fairly consistent in the use of parallel lines of stars.

Even as late as 1876, when Colorado became the thirty-eighth state to join the Union, a bill had not been passed providing for the placement of stars in the flag's canton. It was suggested that the canton should be enlarged and extended to the bottom of the flag. This would mean that a rectangle from top to bottom on the flag's staff side would house the stars.

The problem with this idea was that this would make the flag look the same flown upside down as it would right side up. A flag flown upside down is a signal of distress. If the captain of a ship at sea was in trouble, he could fly his flag upside down and other ships would come to his rescue. So the idea of enlarging the canton to hold all of the stars had to be forgotten.

On October 26, 1912, President Taft issued an executive order that the states (there were then forty-eight of them) should be represented on the flag by six horizontal rows of eight stars each. At last, after many years of indecision, the placement of stars was official! The fifty stars of today's flag follow Taft's rule of arrangement by rows. Today the U.S. flag has five rows of six stars alternating with four rows of five stars. Added together, this totals fifty stars, one for each state.

The Stars and Stripes—or *Old Glory*, as our flag is sometimes called—blends a reminder of the past with pride in the present. Each state in the nation is represented by a star. The last star, for Hawaii, was added in 1959. These stars denote the growth of the nation up to the present time.

But the red and white stripes are a reminder to us of our past history. They recall the original thirteen colonies that began the fight for independence. These stripes symbolize the courage and strength of many men and women who gave their lives in the struggle for freedom. Because of their brave efforts, we can live with pride in our past and hope in the future for our nation, the United States of America.

A GUIDE TO STATE FLAGS

A state represents itself through the colors and symbols found on its flag. For example, a state might use a picture of a bear to symbolize its wildlife. Or a state flag might picture one tree to symbolize the state's many forests. Colors used on flags tend to stand for certain ideas or images. A symbol or color representing something in one flag can symbolize the very same thing in another flag. This guide will help you to recognize some of the symbols in our state flags. Let's begin with colors.

COLORS

Red Red symbolizes courage. In many of the flags, it stands for the blood of patriots shed in their fight for freedom.

White White symbolizes purity. It stands for high moral goals and simplicity.

Blue Blue in a flag is sometimes called "True Blue" or "Loyal Blue." It stands for loyalty and friendship. Blue conveys truth, justice, and honor.

Red, White, and Blue These colors are found in our national flag. Together they stand for patriotism and national pride.

Green Green symbolizes growth and freshness. It often represents environmental concerns and respect for nature. It also symbolizes new or renewed life.

OTHER SYMBOLS

Thirteen A quantity of thirteen symbolizes honor for the original thirteen colonies or states.

Stars Stars usually represent states. Thirteen stars represent the original thirteen colonies. If a state flag has only *one* star, the single star symbolizes the state itself.

Eagle The American bald eagle is our national emblem. On a flag, it represents courage, patriotism, strength, and loyalty to the nation.

Eagle Holding Arrows This image symbolizes the state's readiness to defend itself or the nation in the cause of justice.

Rising Sun This image represents a new age and hope for the future.

Southern Cross or St. Andrew's Cross This is a white-rimmed blue cross containing thirteen white stars. This cross was featured on the battle flag of the Confederate states during the Civil War (War between the States). It is found in miniature on the state flag of some southern states. The white rim around the cross symbolizes the church. This cross on a flag represents respect for the rich heritage of the South.

USEFUL DEFINITIONS

Coat of Arms A shield-like shape that contains pictures, mottoes, and symbols. A coat of arms symbolizes the historical past of the state.

State Seal A state seal is usually round. It contains pictures, symbols, and mottoes, related to a particular place.

Canton The rectangular area on the upper left corner of a flag.

Field The background color of the flag.

DELAWARE

DECEMBER 7, 1787

Became a State: December 7, 1787
Capital: Dover
Flag Adopted: June 13, 1955

Delaware, the First State, features a buff-colored diamond on its flag, which accounts for its other nickname, the Diamond State. The blue and buff colors were originally chosen for the flag because they were the colors that General George Washington chose for the Delaware soldiers' uniforms during the Revolutionary War.

Two men stand within the diamond looking at each other. One appears to be a farmer or a man of the land, holding a hoe. The other is a state rifleman. The two together symbolize cooperation and achievement. Below them appears the state motto, "Liberty and independence."

Before it became a state, Delaware was made up of three small counties which were part of Pennsylvania. The flag's shield is divided into three colored parts, each of which represents one of these original counties.

17

PENNSYLVANIA

Became a State:
 December 12, 1787
Capital: Harrisburg
Flag Adopted: June 13, 1907

The state's coat of arms is centered in Pennsylvania's flag. The two black horses rearing up on either side symbolize strength and usefulness. They stand on a gold base through which is looped a red streamer proclaiming the state's motto, "Virtue, liberty, and independence."

The crossing of a cornstalk and an olive branch under the shield symbolizes a productive and peaceful life. An American eagle atop the shield indicates Pennsylvania's lofty goals and ideals. The shield is divided into three panels. In the top panel is a sailing ship of progress. The plow in the center panel shows the agricultural life. The bottom panel, with its harvested wheat, shows the fruits of the farmer's labor.

NEW JERSEY

Became a State:
  December 18, 1787
Capital: Trenton
Flag Adopted: March 26, 1896

The buff background of New Jersey's flag is the same color found on the uniforms worn by New Jersey soldiers during the Revolutionary War. Buff and blue were chosen for the uniforms because those were the colors of Holland. The original Dutch settlers of New Jersey had immigrated from Holland.

The figure of Liberty stands with her hand gently supporting the state shield. She holds a staff topped by a cap of freedom. Helping her is Ceres, the goddess of agriculture. Ceres holds a cornucopia filled with colorful fruit symbolizing the state's prosperity. The shield pictures three different types of plows used by the colonial farmer. Above the shield is the profile of a horse's head, which portrays strength, speed, and usefulness.

GEORGIA

Became a State:
January 2, 1788
Capital: Atlanta
Flag Adopted: July 1, 1956

Two-thirds of Georgia's flag is occupied by the battle flag of the Confederacy, also known as the Southern Cross. The cross signifies Georgia's pride in its southern heritage and respect for a historically rich past. The red, white, and blue colors stand for purity, courage, and loyalty.

The flag's other third contains Georgia's state seal set against a dark blue background. The seal shows three pillars which stand for Wisdom, Justice, and Moderation. The pillars support an arch which represents the United States Constitution. The pillars also symbolize the three branches of government: legislative, judicial, and executive. A Minuteman stands ready with drawn sword to defend the Constitution.

CONNECTICUT

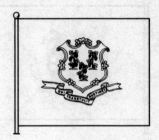

Became a State: January 9, 1788
Capital: Hartford
Flag Adopted: June 3, 1897

The white shield of Connecticut's flag houses three intertwined grapevines. Below the shield, a streamer proclaims the state motto, "Qui transtulit sustinet." This Latin phrase means "Who transplanted will sustain." The motto refers to the original people of the Connecticut colony. They transplanted (moved) themselves from the Massachusetts Bay Colony to three small communities on the Connecticut River. These communities later became known as the Connecticut Colony. The colonists found wild grapes and other fruit growing in Connecticut, which helped them to stay alive. They had not had this advantage in Europe, where grapes were planted by farmers and were not free for others to pick. The colonizers were religious and wanted to show in their state motto their thanks to God for moving them to a land of plenty.

MASSACHUSETTS

Became a State:
  February 6, 1788
Capital: Boston
Flag Adopted:
  March 6, 1915

The Massachusetts state flag is different from many other state flags because it is two-sided, with the same image appearing on both sides. A golden Indian, or Native American, stands against a blue shield. A silver star beside the Indian's head represents the state of Massachusetts. An arm of gold, holding a sword, rises from above the shield. A blue ribbon under the shield proclaims the state motto, "Ense petit placidam sub libertate quietem." The Latin words mean "By the sword we seek peace, but peace only under liberty."

MARYLAND

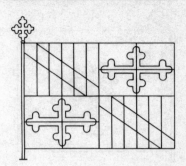

Became a State:
  April 28, 1788
Capital: Annapolis
Flag Adopted: March 9, 1904

The state flag of Maryland has a simple design: four equal-sized rectangles. Within each rectangle is a richly colored pattern that is repeated in the rectangle of the opposite corner. Two of the rectangles are red and white with a *fleur-de-lis* (lily flower) design. These panels suggest a strong religious faith. They also represent the coat of arms of the Crossland family, one of the founding families of Maryland.

The other founding family, the Calvert family, is represented by its coat of arms, a gold and black diamond.

With these symbols of founding families, Maryland's state flag stands for knighthood, religious devotion, and a sense of morality and tradition.

SOUTH CAROLINA

Became a State:
May 23, 1788
Capital: Columbia
Flag Adopted:
January 28, 1861

The blue background of this flag was chosen because the South Carolina soldiers wore blue uniforms during the Revolutionary War. Against this blue field lies a white crescent moon in the upper left corner. A white palmetto tree in the center of the flag was chosen because Fort Sullivan was built of palmetto logs and sand. This fort stood on an island off of South Carolina's coast, and the British attacked it from the sea. The British fired cannons from their ships, but the soft palmetto logs didn't shatter when hit by cannonballs. The fort withstood the pounding and the British sailed away in the middle of the night. The palmetto tree is a fitting symbol of strength and loyalty.

NEW HAMPSHIRE

Became a State: June 21, 1788
Capital: Concord
Flag Adopted: January 1, 1932

The New Hampshire state flag features the state seal against a blue background. Around the seal is a wreath of golden laurel interspersed with nine stars. New Hampshire was the ninth state to join the Union. Within the state seal is a picture of the ship *Raleigh,* one of the first ships in America's navy, getting ready to sail. The ship is docked on a granite boulder for repairs. (New Hampshire is known as the Granite State.) The flag of the United Colonies flies from the ship's stern. The *Raleigh* was the first ship to raise the United Colonies flag. New Hampshire's state flag symbolizes the shipbuilding industry, progress, and hope for the future.

VIRGINIA

Became a State: June 26, 1788
Capital: Richmond
Flag Adopted: April 30, 1861

The Virginia flag is a deep blue color against which is set the state's coat of arms. Virginia is represented by Virtue, a woman dressed as a warrior. She has her foot placed firmly on the chest of her fallen enemy, Tyranny. A broken chain is in Tyranny's left hand, and his golden crown has fallen from his head. Virtue holds the weapons of her victory in her hands. The image represents the surrender of England to the Colonial forces after the Revolutionary War.

Virginia's motto, "Sic semper tyrannis," is printed underneath Tyranny. The motto means "Thus always to tyrants." A wreath of red flowers with green fruit surrounds the seal. It symbolizes the joy, peace, and happiness which come from defeating an oppressor in fair battle.

NEW YORK

Became a State:
  July 26, 1788

Capital: Albany

Flag Adopted:
  April 2, 1901

The New York flag sets the state shield against a background of blue. This shield shows a golden sun rising behind three snow-covered mountains. This scene depicts the natural beauty of New York. A large ship and smaller sloop sail on blue water at the base of the mountains, indicating progress and activity.

On one side of the shield stands Liberty, beautiful and triumphant, with the defeated crown of royalty at her feet. This symbolizes the colonies' victory in their fight against the domination of Great Britian's King George III. On the top of Liberty's staff is a golden cap of freedom. Justice stands by the shield's other side. A scroll under the shield proclaims the state motto, "Excelsior," which means "Ever upward."

NORTH CAROLINA

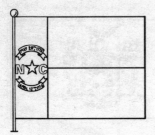

Became a State:
November 21, 1789
Capital: Raleigh
Flag Adopted: March 9, 1885

The North Carolina flag is made up of the same red, white, and blue colors found in the national flag.

A lone white star in the center of the blue area represents the state of North Carolina. A golden scroll above the star proclaims the date that the people of North Carolina declared their independence from Great Britain. North Carolinians still celebrate this day as a legal holiday every year.

The date on the scroll beneath the star is the day that North Carolina cast its vote at the Continental Congress in Philadelphia. North Carolina voted in favor of being loyal to the colonies rather than to Great Britain. The thirteen states had difficulty reaching a decision on this question, and North Carolina paved the way for them to vote for independence.

RHODE ISLAND

Became a State: May 29, 1790
Capital: Providence
Flag Adopted: May 19, 1897

Rhode Island, a state on the Atlantic coast, has a flag that proclaims the state's seafaring history. The anchor is a symbol of Rhode Island from as far back as 1647. Rhode Island was the last of the original thirteen colonies to join the Union. Rhode Island secured the boundaries of the new nation, just as an anchor secures a ship in the ocean waters. The golden anchor is an appropriate symbol for our smallest state.

Rhode Island worked as hard as the twelve larger states during colonial times, hoping for freedom from foreign rule. "Hope" is the state motto written in gold and surrounded by thirteen stars, one for each original colony. The background is pure white.

VERMONT

Became a State:
March 4, 1791
Capital: Montpelier
Flag Adopted:
March 26, 1923

Vermont's coat of arms is displayed against a blue background. The big green pine in the beautiful landscape of the shield depicts Vermont's nickname, the Green Mountain State. The pine branches on the shield's sides represent the Vermonter's Badge. Soldiers from Vermont wore this badge in the 1814 Battle of Plattsburgh against the British during the War of 1812. The cow under the tree represents the state's dairy industry. The three stacks of golden grain stand for Vermont's agricultural industry.

The stag's head above the shield symbolizes abundant wildlife and natural strength. This wildlife kept the first settlers alive during the long, lonely, snowy winter seasons.

The state's motto is displayed in a red scroll under the shield. The motto, "Vermont, freedom and unity," means freedom from oppressors and unity with fellow countrymen and women.

KENTUCKY

Became a State:
June 1, 1792

Capital: Frankfort

Flag Adopted:
March 26, 1918

The Kentucky flag contains an ageless message for all citizens of the United States: "United we stand, divided we fall." This motto, printed on the white state seal, represents the Kentuckians' hope that we will all work together for peace. The seal is set against a navy blue background. Two branches of goldenrod accent the lower half of the seal.

Two friends greet each other on the seal. One man is dressed in frontier clothes, a buckskin outfit originally associated with American Indians. He represents home, hearth, and living on the land. The friend whose hand he shakes appears to be a city gentleman. The two together symbolize cooperation and a combining of different life-styles which make up the state of Kentucky.

TENNESSEE

Became a State: June 1, 1796
Capital: Nashville
Flag Adopted: April 17, 1905

Tennessee was the last state to be granted statehood during the 1700s. Tennessee's flag sports a white-rimmed blue circle against a red background. Within this circle are three white stars representing the state's geographic divisions:

(1) The eastern area, including the state's highest places, part of the Appalachian mountains.
(2) The central region of valleys and plains.
(3) The western area, which includes a band of lowland beside the Mississippi River.

The circle containing the stars represents the unity of the three areas. They are together forever. The red of the flag stands for courage and for the blood spilled in the fight for freedom. The blue strip on the end denotes loyalty and honesty.

OHIO

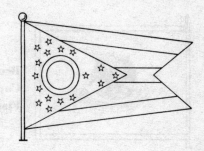

Became a State:
 March 1, 1803
Capital: Columbus
Flag Adopted: May 9, 1902

The flag of Ohio has the only "swallow-tailed" design of all the fifty states. A flag with this shape is called a *burgee*. The Ohio burgee has the same red, white, and blue colors as the national flag. Its red and white stripes represent Ohio's roads and rivers. The blue triangle represents the rolling Ohioan hills. The seventeen white stars within the blue triangle symbolize the first seventeen states of the Union.

The white-rimmed red circle within the blue triangle stands for the first letter of Ohio. It also symbolizes the buckeye, a tree which grows in Ohio. The seed of the buckeye tree was thought by native Indians to look like the eye of a buck. Ohio is nicknamed the Buckeye State.

LOUISIANA

Became a State: April 30, 1812
Capital: Baton Rouge
Flag Adopted: July 1, 1912

The pelican, a water bird, can be found near the marshlands, bayous, and sea coasts of Louisiana. It is a fitting symbol for the Louisiana state flag. The pelican is set against a background of blue. The bird spreads her wings to protect her three chicks as she feeds them. She guards their lives and cares about their health. The image symbolizes the desire of Louisiana citizens to give and share with one another in order that the state and the nation thrive.

The words on the white scroll beneath the nest read, "Union, justice and confidence." This motto suggests that these three things are needed to live a fulfilling life.

INDIANA

Became a State:
  December 11, 1816
Capital: Indianapolis
Flag Adopted: May 31, 1917

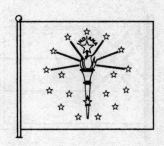

The blue and gold flag of Indiana is a striking combination of color and pattern. Against the blue background are nineteen golden stars which represent the nineteen states in the Union when Indiana became a state. The thirteen stars in the outer circle represent each of the thirteen original states. The largest star, above the flaming torch, represents Indiana. The flaming liberty torch stands for freedom and knowledge.

MISSISSIPPI

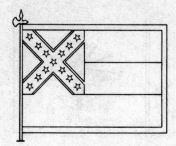

Became a State:
December 10, 1817
Capital: Jackson
Flag Adopted: February 7, 1894

Mississippi's flag bears the same red, white, and blue colors that are found in the national flag. In the upper left-hand corner is a miniature Confederate battle flag. Thirteen stars appear in the blue cross. Each star represents one of the thirteen southern states.

The top bar of blue denotes loyalty and friendship. The white bar beneath stands for purity and high moral outlook. The bottom longer red bar symbolizes courage and the blood of soldiers willing to fight for their ideals and for the independence of their state during the Civil War.

ILLINOIS

Became a State:
  December 3, 1818
Capital: Springfield
Flag Adopted: July 1, 1970

ILLINOIS

Our national emblem, the American bald eagle, is featured on the Illinois state flag. The eagle stands strong and capable upon a solid rock and a patriotic shield. It represents the United States of America as well as the single state of Illinois. The eagle waves a red banner in its beak. The banner proclaims the state motto, "State sovereignty, national union." This means that Illinois is strong and brave enough to stand alone for its rights. But the Prairie State is also loyal enough to come to the defense of the entire nation, if necessary.

The date on the rock, 1818, refers to the year that Illinois became a state. The other date on the rock, 1868, is the year that the current state seal was approved.

The flag was first adopted in 1915. The present flag was officially adopted in 1970. The banner now bears the state seal emblem in color and the word "Illinois."

ALABAMA

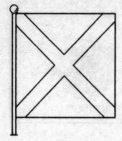

Became a State: December 14, 1819
Capital: Montgomery
Flag Adopted: February 16, 1895

The Alabama flag is simple yet striking. The flag itself is square. The red St. Andrew's cross is the same cross that is found on the Confederate battle flag. Set against a field of pure white, the cross stands out bold and bright, a symbol of courage.

The flag of the Cotton State represents the pride that Alabamians have in their state's rich, historical past. The St. Andrew's cross pays respect to the southern flag of yesteryear. But the boldness and simplicity of design announce change, courage, and individualism for today.

MAINE

Became a State: March 15, 1820
Capital: Augusta
Flag Adopted: February 24, 1909

On Maine's flag the state shield is set against a blue background. The shield shows a peaceful landscape. A moose resting between a blue lake and a large pine tree depicts Maine's natural beauty.

To the left of the shield stands a farmer who grows food from the soil. On the right is a sailor who gathers food from Maine's Atlantic coast. Both of these men symbolize Maine's abundant natural resources and ability to survive. The North Star topping the coat of arms signifies the Maine of 1820 when it was the northernmost state. Under the star is the motto "Dirigo," which means "I direct." This refers to the North Star, which is traditionally used by sailors for navigational purposes. The flag represents a state with respect for its natural beauty and courage to move in directions.

MISSOURI

Became a State:
August 10, 1821
Capital: Jefferson City
Flag Adopted:
March 13, 1913

Patriotic red, white, and blue bars are the background for the coat of arms on Missouri's state flag. A band of twenty-four stars encircles the seal. This represents the twenty-four states of the Union which existed on August 10, 1821, when Missouri became a state. Two grizzly bears, representing the strength and dependability of Missouri citizens, stand on a ribbon that proclaims "Salus populi suprema lex esto." That means "Let the good [or welfare] of the people be the supreme law."

The bears are holding a shield bearing the words "United we stand, divided we fall." The shield shows three sections. One section houses the American eagle, our national emblem. Another section contains a crescent moon which represents Missouri. The third section has a bear which symbolizes the abundant fur trade and wildlife of Missouri in 1821.

ARKANSAS

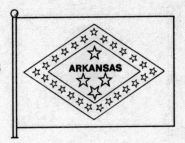

Became a State: June 15, 1836
Capital: Little Rock
Flag Adopted: April 4, 1924

The flag of Arkansas consists of the national red, white, and blue colors. The white diamond in the flag's center symbolizes the fact that Arkansas is the only state in the nation where diamonds are mined as a natural resource.

The large blue star above the state name is a reminder of the Confederacy and of the role Arkansas played during this time in American history. The three blue stars in the bottom of the diamond represent the three countries of which Arkansas has been a possession: Spain, France, and finally, the United States.

MICHIGAN

Became a State:
January 26, 1837
Capital: Lansing
Flag Adopted: April 29, 1911

The Latin words "Si quaeris peninsulam, amoenam circumspice" on Michigan's flag mean "If you seek a pleasant peninsula, look around you." This motto is echoed in the scenic picture on the shield. A frontiersman dressed in buckskin stands on the peninsula. Above him the word "Tuebor" means "I will defend." Holding a musket, he stands ready to defend his state and nation.

The American eagle, carrying arrows in one claw, symbolizes preparedness. Peace is represented by the olive branch in the eagle's other claw. The thirteen olives represent the original thirteen states.

On a red ribbon is the national motto, "E pluribus unum." This Latin phrase means "From many, one." This is a declaration from Michigan that the state will work with other states in peace and cooperation for the good of the entire nation.

FLORIDA

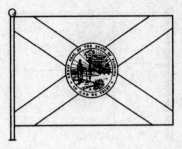

Became a State: March 3, 1845

Capital: Tallahassee

Flag Adopted:
November 6, 1900

A Seminole Indian maiden drops flowers on Florida's coast on the state flag's seal. She is an appropriate symbol of the state because the Seminole tribe is native to Florida. Before the American Revolution, eastern Florida's sparse population was made up chiefly of American Indians. A palm tree on the seal symbolizes the state's subtropical climate. Florida is known as the Sunshine State.

The red cross on the flag resembles the St. Andrew's cross on the Confederate battle flag. This cross echoes Florida's history as a southern state. There were 15,000 Floridian soldiers in the Confederate army.

A steamboat on the water against the backdrop of a rising sun indicates progress. On the bottom of the seal is the state motto, "In God we trust."

TEXAS

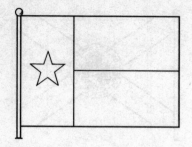

Became a State:
December 29, 1845
Capital: Austin
Flag Adopted:
January 25, 1839

The simple and striking Texas flag is made up of three equal-sized rectangles in red, white, and blue. The red stands for courage, the white suggests strength, and the blue symbolizes loyalty. Each rectangle touches the other two. This signifies mutual dependence on one another for bravery, loyalty, and purity. Against the blue rectangle is a large white star evoking the state's nickname of the Lone Star State.

IOWA

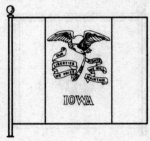

Became a State: December 28, 1846
Capital: Des Moines
Flag Adopted: March 29, 1921

The Iowa state flag consists of a background of three vertical bars of red, white, and blue. This design is similar to France's national flag. The design shows the French influence on Iowa in its early years when France claimed Iowa as part of the Louisiana Territory.

Iowa's flag was designed by Dixie Cornell Gebhardt. She placed the American eagle, our national emblem, in the flag's center. The eagle carries in its mouth a banner with the state motto: "Our liberties we prize, and our rights we will maintain."

WISCONSIN

Became a State: May 29, 1848
Capital: Madison
Flag Adopted: April 26, 1913

Wisconsin's coat of arms is set against the deep blue field of its state flag. Beside the shield stands a sailor who represents Wisconsin's water-related industry. Supporting the seal on the other side is a miner who earns his daily bread from his labor on the land. The four symbols within the seal indicate four major ways of earning a living in Wisconsin during the 1800s. The plow represents Wisconsin's farm and dairy industry. The pick and shovel indicate the mining industry, the anchor stands for the state's water activities, and the strong arm in the lower section represents Wisconsin's industrial success.

A badger is on top of the shield. He represents early miners who made their homes by building underground huts that resembled badger holes. Today Wisconsin is sometimes known as the Badger State.

CALIFORNIA

Became a State:
  September 9, 1850
Capital: Sacramento
Flag Adopted:
  February 3, 1911

On June 14, 1846, a group of American pioneers revolted against Mexican control in California. They pulled down the defeated Mexican flag in Sonoma and replaced it with a hastily made flag of their own. The grizzly bear featured on the flag has remained basically the same to this day. The California grizzly bear, now extinct, is a symbol of determination.

Legend says that a woman in Sonoma offered her red flannel petticoat to be used for the red bar at the bottom of California's first flag. This red bar represents the courage needed to fight for one's freedom and the willingness to achieve goals through combined effort. The flag's star represents the Golden State of California.

MINNESOTA

Became a State: May 11, 1858
Capital: St. Paul
Flag Adopted: April 4, 1893

The nineteen golden stars around Minnesota's state seal indicate that Minnesota was the nineteenth state to join the union after the original thirteen states. The largest yellow star at the top represents Minnesota. In 1858, Minnesota took Maine's place as the northernmost state, giving rise to its nickname, the North Star State.

The state seal is against a blue background. It depicts a pioneer farmer working the land for a living. The farmer watches an American Indian riding a horse into the sunset. This rider symbolizes a new beginning for the state. Minnesota's state flower, the lady's slipper, makes a lovely green and red wreath around the seal. A red banner proclaims in French, "L'Etoile du Nord," which means "the star of the north."

OREGON

Became a State:
February 14, 1859

Capital: Salem

Flag Adopted:
February 26, 1925

Oregon's flag is different from most other state flags because it is two-sided. The front side of the flag has thirty-three golden stars around the state shield. This represents each state in the nation at the time of Oregon's statehood. Oregon became the thirty-third state on St. Valentine's Day in 1859.

The covered wagon pulled by oxen represents the pioneering spirit of Oregon in the 1800s. The trees and elk behind the wagon portray the beautiful forests and wildlife in Oregon. Two ships can be seen. One, a British ship, is sailing away. The other, an American steamer, is headed for shore with determination. The two ships symbolize the end of British influence and the rise of American power. The state motto, "The Union," refers to the unity and loyalty among the states.

On the flag's reverse side is a golden beaver, which symbolizes the state's wildlife.

KANSAS

Became a State:
January 29, 1861

Capital: Topeka

Flag Adopted:
March 21, 1927

A scene of Kansas in the 1800s is pictured within the flag's seal. A rising sun promises a new day in which to grow and change. A steamboat, up with the morning sun and already at work, chugs down the river. A Kansas farmer is also at work, plowing the fertile farmland.

Two covered wagons bring early settlers to a new life in Kansas. Two American Indian hunters on horseback chase a heard of buffalo that once thrived on the Kansas prairie. The Kansas motto, "Ad astra per aspera," means "To the stars through difficulties." This means that no matter what obstacles lie ahead of them, people from Kansas are prepared to deal with them in order to attain their goals.

The sunflower above the seal grows wild in Kansas and gives Kansas its nickname, the Sunflower State.

WEST VIRGINIA

Became a State:
June 20, 1863

Capital: Charleston

Flag Adopted:
March 7, 1929

The Mountain State flag is pure white bordered with blue. The state seal shows a rock bearing the date of statehood. Beside the rock stands a farmer holding a woodsman's ax. This scene depicts the hard task that pioneers faced. The pioneers had to clear forests in order to build homes and towns. The corn beside the farmer and the wheat at his feet show his work and success at farming. A miner, pickax in hand, represents the mining industry, which has always been an important business in West Virginia.

Two hunting rifles are crossed in the foreground with a cap of freedom upon them. This indicates the freedom of West Virginia which was won by force from the state of Virginia during the Civil War. The words "Montani semper liberi" are on a red ribbon below the guns. The words mean "Mountaineers are always free."

NEVADA

Became a State:
  October 31, 1864
Capital: Carson City
Flag Adopted: March 26, 1929

The flag of the Silver State is an appropriate gun-metal blue, bearing the words "Battle Born" as a reminder that Nevada gained statehood during the Civil War. The United States acquired the land that became Nevada after our war with Mexico (1846 to 1848). Many battles were fought during this struggle. Nevada became a state in 1864, when the Civil War was raging. As pioneers moved into the state, they were often engaged in battles with the resident American Indian tribes. The people of Nevada have an early history of fighting for their freedom and their state.

In the flag's upper left corner is a single star representing Nevada. Beneath the star are two sprigs of sagebrush, which were used by Indians in their healing medicine. Sagebrush is the state flower.

NEBRASKA

Became a State:
  March 1, 1867
Capital: Lincoln
Flag Adopted:
  March 28, 1925

Nebraska was the first state to join the Union after the Civil War. A smith in the foreground of the state seal hammers on a golden anvil. This workman symbolizes the hardworking, industrious citizens of Nebraska. Sheaves of golden wheat and corn around the settler's cabin represent the agricultural contributions of the Cornhusker State. The flag's background of dark blue sets off the gold and sliver colors in the seal.

Behind the smith, a steamship paddles up the Missouri River. A train beside the river carries Nebraska's produce and beef to the rest of the country and the world. The Rocky Mountains on the state's extreme west side stand behind a scene of bustling activity and industry. The state motto, "Equality before the law," crowns this portrait of the state.

COLORADO

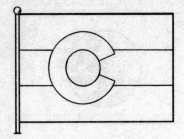

Became a State:
August 1, 1876
Capital: Denver
Flag Adopted: March 31, 1964

A patriotic combination of red, white, and blue is found in the flag of the Centennial State. The large red *C* can stand for Colorado, Centennial, or the Columbine State (columbine is the state flower). The red color of the *C* can also represent the color of Colorado's soil. In Spanish, *colorado* means "ruddy" or "reddish."

The gold disk within the *C* represents Colorado's rich gold mines. The Gold Rush to the West included Colorado, where large deposits of gold were discovered in the Rockies by adventurous prospectors. This precious metal encouraged new settlers and greatly influenced the growth of the state.

The top and bottom bars of the flag are the same shade of blue that can be found in the national flag.

NORTH DAKOTA

Became a State:
  November 2, 1889
Capital: Bismarck
Flag Adopted: March 3, 1911

North Dakota's patriotic flag features our national emblem, the American eagle. The desire for peace is symbolized in the olive branch carried in its claw. The arrows in the other talons indicate a readiness for battle if all attempts at peace have been exhausted. The arrows may also represent the seven American Indian tribes of North Dakota: the Sioux (North Dakota's nickname is the Sioux State), Mandan, Arikara, Hidatsa, Chippewa, Cheyenne, and Assiniboine.

In the eagle's mouth is a ribbon proclaiming our national motto, "E pluribus unum," which means "from many, one." The eagle carries its national message against a background of blue, representing the First North Dakota Infantry.

SOUTH DAKOTA

Became a State:
November 2, 1889
Capital: Pierre
Flag Adopted: March 8, 1909

On South Dakota's state flag, its nickname, the Sunshine State, is printed in golden letters under the state seal. The scene portrayed in this seal is one of life in South Dakota in earlier times. A farmer guides the plow behind his horses. His farmlands stretch into the distance and contain a herd of cattle and rows of crops. With hard work, his life is a prosperous one.

A steamboat symbolizes transportation, and a furnace on the river's other side represents South Dakota's mining industry.

The seal is surrounded by a halo of golden rays of the sun. The flag's background color is an azure blue, the color of the sky on a clear, sunshiny day.

MONTANA

Became a State: November 8, 1889
Capital: Helena
Flag Adopted: February 27, 1905

The beauty of Montana's landscape is portrayed in the state seal on its blue flag. It shows an orange sun rising in a golden sky with promises of a bright day. Gray mountains reflect the sun's rosy light. A silvery waterfall rushes into a blue-tinted lake and keeps the surrounding vegetation lush and green. The scene sings a praise to Montana's natural beauty.

On Montana's flag is the state motto, "Oro y plata." This Spanish phrase means "gold and silver." The motto refers to a gold strike in Montana in 1862, which tempted adventure-seeking settlers into the state. These early settlers founded Montana's prosperous mining industry.

The farming, ranching, and mining tools above the motto indicate a variety of occupations pursued by Montana's first settlers.

WASHINGTON

Became a State:
  November 11, 1889
Capital: Olympia
Flag Adopted: March 5, 1923

The state flag of Washington pays respect to our nation's founding father, George Washington. The portrait of our first president is set against a field of dark green. This green represents the lush forests of the Evergreen State and refers to the state's environmental concerns.

The flag was designed by the Talcott brothers who lived in Olympia, the state capital. The brothers were silversmiths who owned and worked in the oldest jewelry store in the state.

By featuring General Washington on the state flag and naming their state after him, the citizens of Washington proclaim their intent to follow the guiding principles of honesty, sincerity, and devotion commonly associated with our first president.

IDAHO

Became a State: June 3, 1890
Capital: Boise
Flag Adopted: March 15, 1927

The designer of Idaho's state flag, Mrs. J. G. Green, lived during a time when women were just beginning to join together in their fight for voting rights. With this in mind, she placed a figure of a woman in an equal position of importance with a man on the state seal. The woman represents liberty and justice. The man represents industry, particularly mining. The cornucopias at the figures' feet represent Idaho's prosperous agricultural industry.

A picture of Idaho's countryside is depicted in the shield. An elk's head above the shield signifies that moose and elk are protected by Idaho's game laws.

The scroll at the top of the seal proclaims "Esto perpetua," which means "may she endure forever." These words indicate the hope that the natural loveliness of Idaho and of the nation will last forever.

WYOMING

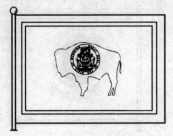

Became a State: July 10, 1890
Capital: Cheyenne
Flag Adopted: January 31, 1917

The western custom of cattle branding comes to mind as one views the Wyoming flag with its state seal set against the outline of a buffalo. In the seal a woman on a pedestal holds a banner which declares "Equal Rights." This refers to the equal political and voting status women have held with men since the beginning of the Equality State. Two men stand in support of equality. One man with a lasso in his hand, symbolizes Wyoming's history of cattle herds, rodeos, ranching, and livestock. Another nickname for Wyoming is the Cowboy State.

The other man, leaning on a pickax, represents Wyoming's prosperous mining industry. Mining has been an important source of income in the state since its early days.

UTAH

Became a State:
  January 4, 1896
Capital: Salt Lake City
Flag Adopted: March 11, 1913

The beehive pictured on Utah's state flag represents hard work and productive activity. Native sego lilies, which symbolize peace and survival, grow beside the hive. These white flowers provided early pioneers with beauty as well as with food. Livestock and game were scarce for Utah's pioneers who were trying to make a living by farming the land. The roots of the sego lily could be cooked and eaten and were often daily fare in a Utah pioneer's meal.

The national flags draped in the shield represent Utah's loyalty to the entire nation. Under them, the date 1847 appears. This date commemorates the year that Brigham Young and his Mormon followers claimed Utah's lands as their home.

OKLAHOMA

Became a State:
November 16, 1907
Capital: Oklahoma City
Flag Adopted: April 2, 1925

The sky-blue background of Oklahoma's flag represents wide open spaces, fresh air, clear skies, and friendship. Centered against this blue background is an American Indian war shield with six crosses on its face. The cross was an Indian symbol for stars, and stars stood for high hopes and goals. The eagle feathers hanging from the shield represent the many American Indian tribes living in Oklahoma at the time of statehood, including the Cherokee, Chickasaw, Choctaw, Creek, and Seminole.

Across the shield lies an Indian peace pipe. On top of the pipe is an olive branch, the white man's symbol for peace. Together they indicate the strength of friendship that can be forged between people of different races and cultures. Oklahoma's state flag suggests hope for peace between all people.

NEW MEXICO

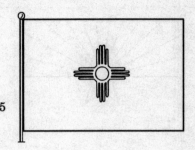

Became a State:
  January 6, 1912
Capital: Santa Fe
Flag Adopted: March 19, 1925

The red design on New Mexico's flag is a symbol for the sun. This symbol was used by the Indians of Zia Pueblo. American Indians, New Mexico's first inhabitants, worshipped the sun's life-giving powers. Ancient Indian civilizations inhabited New Mexico before the first Vikings came ashore in America.

From the sun comes life and growth for people, animals, and plants; without it there would be no life. The sun is a very fitting symbol for the sunshine state, because it has nurtured civilizations in New Mexico, the Land of Enchantment, who sent explorers into the state during the 1500s.

ARIZONA

Became a State:
February 14, 1912

Capital: Phoenix

Flag Adopted:
February 27, 1917

Centered on Arizona's state flag is a star, which represents the state of Arizona and its copper mining industry. It also reminds one of a sheriff's badge worn by a lawman of the Old West. The starburst of seven red and six yellow shafts represents the original thirteen states of the Union. The red and gold colors of the flag are a tribute to the colors of Spain's flag under Queen Isabella (1451 to 1504), who sent Spanish adventurers to explore the land that later became Arizona. These bands of explorers were among the first Europeans to enter this territory.

ALASKA

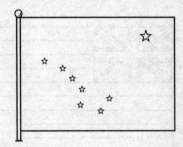

Became a State:
  January 3, 1959
Capital: Juneau
Flag Adopted: May 2, 1927

   Alaska's state flag was designed in 1926 by a seventh-grade student named Benny Benson. He explained that the blue background represents the beautiful Alaskan sky and the state flower, the forget-me-not.

   The golden stars of the Big Dipper, a constellation also known as the Greater Bear, are spread across the flag. This starry cluster represents strength and constancy. The North Star is in the upper right corner of the cluster. The North Star has been traditionally used by explorers in navigating. The vastness and wildness of the Alaskan terrain has tempted many an explorer and adventurer in the search for adventure and wealth. The stars in the night sky have guided them to safety. Alaska, our northernmost state, is represented by this one star of hope and guidance.

HAWAII

Became a State:
August 21, 1959
Capital: Honolulu
Flag Adopted: July 3, 1894

King Kamehameha I of Hawaii was given a British flag by Captain George Vancouver during one of his visits to Hawaii in 1793. Hawaiians had not used flags before this time. Their symbols of authority and identification were called *kahilis,* bird feathers arranged on top of a pole. These poles were carried into battle or used during royal ceremonies. King Kamehameha I wanted his own flag to represent the island, so a new one was designed. But the Union Jack was retained in the canton out of respect to Great Britain. Hawaii is the only state to pay direct tribute to a foreign country in this way. King Kamehameha I unified the Hawaiian islands and placed them under British protection in 1794.

The eight stripes in red, white, and blue represent Hawaii's eight islands: Hawaii, Maui, Oahu, Kauai, Molokai, Lanai, Niihau, and Kahoolawe.

U.S. DEPENDENCIES

The United States has several dependencies, including Guam, the Virgin Islands, and Puerto Rico. A *dependency* is a territory of land under the protection of another country. A dependency is not formally a part of the protecting country.

Each of the U.S. dependencies is an island or cluster of islands. They depend on the United States for their safety and welfare. Each dependency has its own flag which it flies beside the U.S. flag. The Stars and Stripes always occupies the place of honor, which is on your left as you face the flag.

The flag of Guam centers its seal against a dark blue background.The red-trimmed seal is a vertical ellipse which looks like an eye standing on its side. Within the seal is a coastline of Guam's subtropical shore. An outrigger canoe floats in the water, representing the outdoor activities of this island country in the Pacific Ocean. A coconut tree grows out of the sand and up through the name Guam in an artistic design. The tree symbolizes the bounty of the land.

A second U.S. dependency is the Virgin Islands. The islands' inhabitants fly a pure white flag featuring a noble eagle. The eagle grasps three arrows in one claw. This scene symbolizes the pride that the islanders feel in their home and their readiness to defend their home if necessary. The eagle holds an olive branch in its other claw, indicating that the islanders desire peace. The letters V and I flank the eagle on either side.

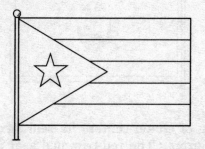

The island of Puerto Rico in the West Indies is another U.S. dependency. Puerto Rico, which means "rich port," was discovered by Columbus on November 19, 1493. Columbus claimed it for Spain and at first named it San Juan Bautista (Spanish for St. John the Baptist). Its name was later changed to Puerto Rico.

Puerto Rico remained a Spanish possession until the end of the Spanish-American War in 1898. It became a dependency of the United States after the signing of the Treaty of Paris in 1899. Since 1952, it has been self-governing, but it remains a U.S. dependency.

The Puerto Rican flag is designed after a flag used by the Puerto Rican patriots of 1895, fighting for their independence from Spain. This group united with a Cuban patriot group who was also fighting for its independence from Spain. Because of these close ties, the Puerto Rican flag is similar to the Cuban flag.

The Puerto Rican flag shows five horizontal bars: two white and three red. These colors represent purity and the courage of a people willing to fight for their liberty.

The blue triangle at the left represents the unity of the people and their loyalty to the island they live on. On the field of blue is a white star symbolizing Puerto Rico.

Whose Flag Am I?

Read what the flag has to say (if flags could talk!). It will give you a hint as you try to guess which state the flag belongs to. If you think you know the state's name, write it in the blank. (The answers are on page 80.)

FLAG

1) I have one white "Lone Star" against a blue background.

   _____

2) The people in my state used to eat roots of sego lilies because meat was scarce. That's why I show the sego lily on my shield.

   _____

3) I'm proud to show a red symbol for the sun against a yellow background. This is an ancient American Indian symbol.

   _____

4) The white diamond on my center symbolizes the fact that I'm the only state where diamonds are mined as a natural resource.

   _____

5) A big, green pine tree represents my beautiful green mountains.

   _____

6) My three pillars (Wisdom, Justice, and Moderation) support an arch (the United States Constitution).

   _____

7) My motto is "Liberty and independence" and I represent the very first state.

_____

8) The two founding families of my state combined their coat of arms to make me.

_____

9) I represent the first state to join the Union after the Civil War. Sheaves of wheat and corn represent my state's farming history.

_____

10) I show two different symbols for peace because the people of my state think it's important for everyone to get along together.

_____

11) My *C* can also stand for "Centennial" and the "Columbine State."

_____

12) During a battle in my state it was discovered that palmetto trees can withstand the pounding of cannonballs. My design depicts a large palmetto tree.

_____

13) Two grizzly bears represent the courage and loyalty of my state's citizens.

_____

14) My bright green color shows pride in my state's forests. And I display a picture of the first president of the United States.

_____

15) I'm the only flag to be shaped into a swallow-tailed design. I'm known as a *burgee*.

_____

16) I show a constellation of stars. And I was designed by a seventh-grade student named Benny Benson.

_____

17) Th early settlers of my state were glad to find wild grapes growing in the forests. I was designed to show three grapevines on my shield.

_____

18) My seal features a woman carrying a banner which says "Equal rights." The men and women of my state are proud to share equal political status.

_____

19) Tyranny lies defeated on the ground, while Virtue stands proudly with her weapons of victory in her hands. She symbolizes the courage that the people of my state showed during the Revolutionary War.

_____

20) I show two friends shaking hands. One is a city gentleman and the other is a frontiersman. My motto says, "United we stand, divided we fall."

_____

Flag Facts

Can you answer these questions about the national flag and its history? Circle the letter of the correct answer after each question. (The answers are on page 80.)

1) The Union Jack is
   a) a kind of cheese.
   b) Spain's flag.
   c) Great Britain's flag.
   d) a kind of flagpole.

2) The number thirteen in a state flag usually stands for
   a) the number of years it takes to become a state.
   b) bad luck.
   c) the number of troops led by George Washington
   d) the original thirteen colonies.

3) The Grand Union is
   a) the uniting of the thirteen colonies against English troops.
   b) the place where General Washington organized his soldiers before crossing the Delaware River.
   c) another name for the Stars and Stripes.
   d) a set of international laws.

4) During colonial times, a ship at sea without a flag was considered to be
   a) a pirate ship.
   b) a slave ship.
   c) lost.
   d) from Spain.

5) The national flag of the United States of America is also known as
   a) the Red, White, and Blue.
   b) the Stars and Stripes.
   c) Old Glory.
   d) a, b, and c.

6) The stars in our nation's flag represent
   a) each state in the Union.
   b) important battles fought during the Revolutionary War.
   c) the number of American presidents.
   d) the number of years that we've had a democracy.

7) The first and last states to join the Union and receive a star were
   a) Georgia and Alaska.
   b) Massachusetts and Montana.
   c) Delaware and Hawaii.
   d) Georgia and New Mexico.

8) The Continental Army led by _____ was formally proclaimed on the same day that a new colonial flag was raised.
   a) Thomas Jefferson
   b) Billy the Kid
   c) George Washington
   d) Francis Scott Key

9) Today's national flag's canton contains
   a) fifty stars.
   b) thirteen stripes.
   c) money to support the military.
   d) George Washington's signature.

10) The Grand Union flying over Fort McHenry during a battle against the British inspired
   a) George Washington to defend Fort McHenry.
   b) many states to want to join the Union.
   c) Francis Scott Key to write "The Star-Spangled Banner."
   d) the burning of the fort.

11) Flags serve the important function of
   a) wind-direction indicators.
   b) leading parades.
   c) identification.
   d) justifying the existence of flagpoles.

12) The national flag flown during the War of 1812 was sewn by
   a) Martha Washington.
   b) leaders of the thirteen original colonies.
   c) Betsy Ross.
   d) Mary Young Pickersgill and her daughter.

13) In 1818, a bill was passed stating that each new state would
   a) be represented by a star on the national flag.
   b) receive a national flag to fly in their capital city.
   c) never be allowed to drop out of the Union.
   d) have to legally define its boundaries.

14) The flag flown during the War of 1812 is now on display
   a) in Boston, Massachusetts.
   b) at the Smithsonian Institution in Washington, D.C.
   c) at Rockefeller Center in New York.
   d) in a cathedral in Coventry, England.

15) The canton in the first Grand Union contained
   a) a circle of thirteen stars.
   b) a small British flag.
   c) red and white stripes.
   d) a rattlesnake with thirteen rattles.

16) When Vermont and Kentucky joined the Union, the number of stars on the national flag grew to
   a) twelve.
   b) fifteen.
   c) seventeen.
   d) twenty.

17) If you saw a ship at sea and its flag was flying upside down, you would know that
   a) the ship and its crew were in trouble and they needed help.
   b) the ship was preparing for battle.
   c) the captain was taking a nap.
   d) a crew member had sighted sharks in the area.

18) As early as 1777, the U.S. Navy was fairly
    constant in the arrangement of the stars on
    its flag into
    a) circles.
    b) one large star.
    c) a diamond shape.
    d) parallel lines.

19) On October 26, 1912, President _____
    issued an executive order which stated the
    official arrangement of stars on the
    national flag.
    a) Taft
    b) Lincoln
    c) Washington
    d) Hoover

Hidden Words

All of the words listed below are hidden in the puzzle. They go up, down, diagonally, and backwards. Circle the words when you find them. The first three are done for you. (Answers are on page 80.)

NATION	STARS AND STRIPES	UNITED
SHIELD	RED WHITE AND BLUE	BURGEE
MOTTO	GRAND UNION	BUCKEYE
CANTON	IN GOD WE TRUST	EMBLEM
EAGLE	COAT OF ARMS	BANNER
SEAL	SYMBOL	STATE
GOLD	SOUTHERN CROSS	THIRTEEN
JUSTICE	COLONIST	STAR
HISTORY	FLAG	INDIAN
	WASHINGTON	SOONER

```
I M E L U O F N I N D I A N B O T
N O J U N T E F R C B G I U P R S
G O U A I E L F T J R H R A S U H
O V S M T N O R E A O G D G O E R
D J T R E R B E N I E O I O U N T
W M I K D A O D A E C B P Z T O A
E H C M B T U W T N O W S Y H T P
T S E S T N S H I E L D Y R E G M
R M Z O I P H I O G O L M O R N I
U R M O D N W T N A N L B T N I A
S A N N M O S E A L I A O S C H D
T F D E A T M A H F S R L I R S E
W O O R P N I N O P T M U H O A Y
S T A R S A N D S T R I P E S W E
H A B A M C L B W V T S A Q S E K
U O E T A T S L A Y R G D L O G C
T C Q U I L M U B R L H S T A R U
N R E N N A B E E E M B L E M A B
```

ANSWERS

Whose Flag Am I?

1) Texas
2) Utah
3) New Mexico
4) Arkansas
5) Vermont
6) Georgia
7) Delaware
8) Maryland
9) Nebraska
10) Oklahoma
11) Colorado
12) South Carolina
13) Missouri
14) Washington
15) Ohio
16) Alaska
17) Connecticut
18) Wyoming
19) Virginia
20) Kentucky

Flag Facts

1) c
2) d
3) c
4) a
5) d
6) a
7) c
8) c
9) a
10) c
11) c
12) d
13) a
14) b
15) b
16) b
17) a
18) d
19) a

Hidden Words

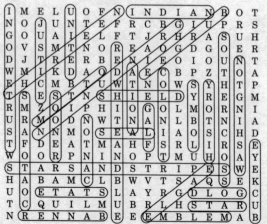

80